Creative
Three-dimensional
Découpage

This book is dedicated to my mum who is a very special lady. She has always given her support and encouragement to all my endeavours. She instilled in me a love of sewing and crafts at a very early age.

I would also like to thank my husband, Tony, and my two boys, Stuart and Jonathan, for their patience and encouragement during the long months of working on the designs for this book.

To my friend Marion I am deeply indebted. I would like to thank her for the time she spent cheerfully cutting out many of the projects. Her enthusiasm was infectious.

My special thanks go to Lesley Teare for painting the beautiful poppy design, prints of which are included at the back of this book.

Finally, I would like to thank Roz Dace for giving me the opportunity to write this book. It has allowed me to develop my ideas to new and inspired levels.

Creative
Three-dimensional
Découpage

DEBBIE SELLERS

SEARCH PRESS

First published in Great Britain 1998

Search Press Limited
Wellwood, North Farm Road,
Tunbridge Wells, Kent TN2 3DR

ISBN 0 85532 836 3

Acknowledgements
The images on pages 1, 28–29, 34–35, 57, 6–61 and 64 have been reproduced with the kind permission of John Arnold Publishing, Fine Art Publishers, of Unit 1B, Forge Way, Brown Lees Industrial Estate, Knypersley, Biddulph, Stoke-on-Trent, England.

The images on pages 1, 27, 28–29, 31, 34–35, 63 and 66 are reproduced with the kind permission of Robin Sudbury Associates of Newstead, Vicarage Lane, Bowdon, Altrincham, Cheshire, England.

Images on pages 1, 3, 5, 6, 7, 25, 28–29, 34–35, 36, 37, 38, 47, 49, 50–51, 53, 55, 56, 62, 65, 67 are reproduced with the kind permission of Manor Art Enterprises Limited of 555 East Boston Post Road, Mammaroneck, New York 10543, USA.

Suppliers
If you have any difficulty in obtaining any of the equipment or materials mentioned in this book, then please write for further information, either to the Publishers:

Search Press Ltd.,
Wellwood, North Farm Road,
Tunbridge Wells, Kent TN2 3DR

or to the author, Debbie Sellers at:

Debbie Crafts
7 Bromham Mill, Giffard Park,
Milton Keynes, Bucks MK14 5QP

Printed in Spain by Elkar S. Coop. Bilbao 48012

Contents

Introduction

Three-dimensional découpage is the fascinating art of making realistic three-dimensional pictures from a number of flat artist's prints. The effect is achieved by cutting, shaping and reassembling the paper pieces to give a three-dimensional image. The design can be finished with glaze to create the look of porcelain and then placed into a deeply recessed frame to give a stunning result.

Little is known about the history of this craft but it is assumed that it evolved from the flat style of découpage which was popular in Venice during the seventeenth century. Heavily lacquered and embellished furniture from China and Japan was very fashionable at that time. The Venetian craftsmen developed a way of copying it by cutting out paper designs and setting them into place under layers of lacquer. The finished result looked as if the detail was inlaid. It was called *arte povero*.

The craft was given the name découpage (from the verb *découper* meaning 'to cut') when it moved to France. Marie Antoinette and her court would spend many happy hours cutting out paper shapes. Sadly, there were no special prints available at that time and so many valuable paintings were destroyed by the ladies practising the craft.

Découpage first arrived in Britain during the Victorian age, and is thought to have been brought back by those returning from their Grand Tour of Europe. The Victorians had a love of elaborate decoration and with the advent of the printing process, books of scraps designed especially for the craft were printed.

The availability of cheaper prints led the way forward for three-dimensional découpage. Initially little shadow boxes were made, with pieces of cork used to separate the layers of the picture. These were called *vue d'optiques*. Modern day découpage can now take advantage of cheap, mass-produced prints and the introduction of silicone glue.

My fascination with découpage is relentless. It is fuelled by the challenge to complete more and more complex designs and to develop new techniques to make them as realistic as possible. In this book I hope to show you a variety of innovative techniques to capture your imagination. However, beware. . . it can become very addictive!

Tools and materials

You can start three-dimensional découpage with a set of prints and just a few other tools and materials – you may already have many of the essential tools around the home; others can be obtained from good art and craft outlets or through mail order.

PRINTS
Mail order suppliers have a large range of prints especially selected for this craft. A more limited range can be found in craft shops. Wrapping papers with repeat designs or cheap greetings cards are good alternatives for the beginner.

CUTTING EQUIPMENT
Good cutting tools are essential. You will need a pair of fine cuticle scissors, preferably with curved blades, and a small craft knife. A self-healing cutting mat is useful to protect surfaces but a scrap piece of mount board makes a good substitute.

GLUES
A silicone glue is used to build up the layers of the picture and give it depth. It is a rubbery solution which holds its shape when dry. Blobs of dried glue can be removed very simply and, if you are unhappy with the finished picture, it can be eased apart and reassembled.

It is also useful to have a glue stick and some PVA glue in your workbox.

PAINTS
The cut-out pieces of paper have white edges which must be coloured before the pieces are assembled. A small palette of watercolour paints and a small brush will serve most needs.

Many prints have a shiny surface that will not take weak colours. If you want to patch out anything on these prints, it is best to use neat colours from tubes of watercolour paints.

MOULDING TOOLS
A soft spongy mat is required to shape each of the paper pieces – a shoe insole or a computer mouse mat is ideal.

Mould shapes with the smooth handle of your scissors or with a balling or burnishing tool.

GLAZES
Special cold glazes are available to give your finished picture the look of porcelain. Do not use anything else – clear nail varnish, for example, will crack and turn yellow in time.

TWEEZERS
A long thin pair of surgical tweezers are essential for handling tiny pieces.

OTHER ITEMS
Cocktail sticks are ideal for transferring blobs of glue from the tube to the picture.

Pieces of sponge can be used with paint to create textured backgrounds for your designs, and to patch out unwanted images.

Paper towelling will help keep your fingers and equipment clean.

Strips of foam board, available from art and craft shops, can be used to raise the foreground areas of deep-recessed pictures and to make boxed-in frames.

Good quality tracing paper, a pencil and paper clips are used for preparing cutting guides.

A selection of mount boards, available from picture framers, can be used as backgrounds for your picture.

Materials for customising your picture with fine details are given on page 26.

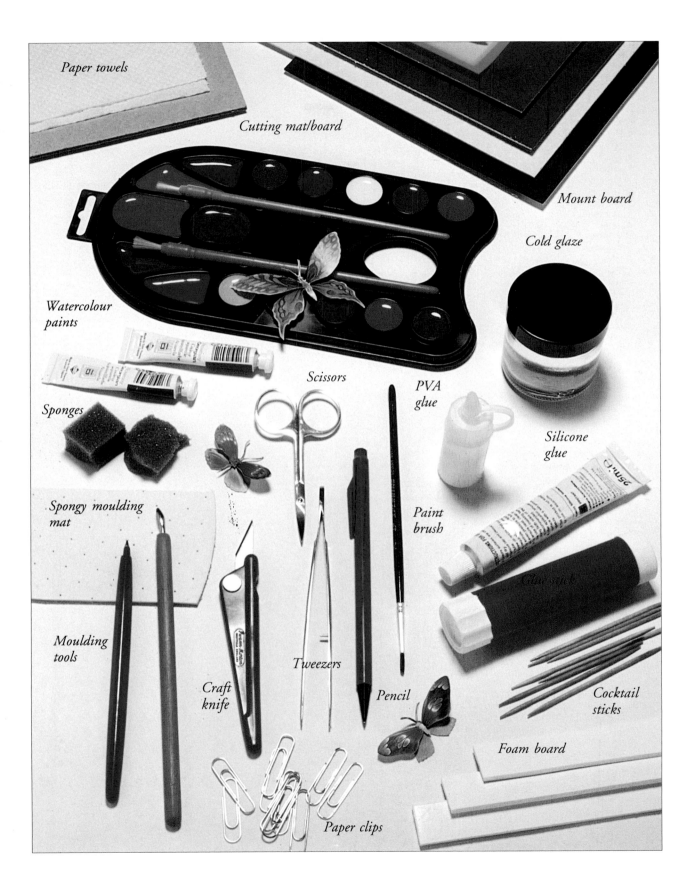

Paper towels

Cutting mat/board

Mount board

Cold glaze

Watercolour
paints

Sponges

Scissors

PVA
glue

Silicone
glue

Spongy moulding
mat

Paint
brush

Glue stick

Moulding
tools

Tweezers

Craft
knife

Pencil

Cocktail
sticks

Foam board

Paper clips

9

Choosing a subject

You must choose your subject carefully if you want to create a successful three-dimensional découpage picture.

The elements of the design must have clearly defined edges to make cutting out easy. Try to avoid images that have blurred edges – watercolour paintings, for example, often have indistinct outlines.

Designs are assembled from the back to the front of the picture, so there must be an obvious back-ground and foreground, with some intermediary layers in between.

Making a good choice comes with experience, so start with simple designs that do not require too many fine pieces. Before buying prints, practise with wrapping paper or cheap greetings cards.

The pansy design below is a good example of a suitable subject. Study the picture and note the various layers. You will see that the sky is a very definite background. Moving forward, there is a

layer of grasses; these are in front of the sky but behind the pansies. The leaves at the bottom of the picture make other layers which mainly lie behind the pansies. The flower heads are all at different levels; each has its own layers of petals, with one final large petal at the front.

When you become aware of these layers, you must plan how to convert them into a three-dimensional image – for this I suggest preparing a set of cutting guides (see pages 12–13).

This study of pansies makes an ideal subject for three-dimensional découpage. The outlined detail is used on pages 12–13 to show how to prepare cutting guides. A three-dimensional image of the complete picture is shown on pages 14–15.

Preparing cutting guides

The first step in any project is the preparation of a set of cutting guides; these will enable you to check that you have sufficient prints to complete the design, and help avoid costly mistakes when you start cutting pieces from the prints. This is the most challenging aspect of three-dimensional découpage and takes some practice. Always begin with a simple design.

Most print suppliers will give advice on the number of prints needed for a particular design, and often sell pre-packed sets of prints. As a general rule, most floral pictures can be cut from five prints. Obviously, the more complex the design the more prints you will require – for example, the landscape project on pages 40–47 requires ten prints.

I love working with pansies: they are brightly coloured; they have a well-defined petal structure; and they look wonderful when assembled. To help explain how I prepare cutting guides I have used a detail from the pansy picture featured on pages 10–11. I have used five prints for this picture; one for the background (the base print), and four from which to cut out the pieces of the design.

To avoid marking the prints, I draw the guides on good quality tracing paper secured to the prints with paper clips. There are no hard and fast rules to follow and the finished guides can vary from person to person. I work from the back of the design, through the intermediary layers, to the front. Do not worry if you are unable to cut the pieces out in the order in which they are assembled – the idea is to use the least number of prints.

Look carefully at one of the pansies opposite and try to identify the five petals that make up the flower head and the order in which they are attached. It may help to look at a real flower head to see how the petals are interleaved. Note how the leaves and grasses lay behind the flowers. Where a petal or leaf is partly hidden by another part of the design, it must be cut with an extra piece (an extension) attached to it. Extensions allow you to assemble the design without obvious joins between overlapping pieces; they also provide areas on to which other layers can be glued.

Outline the flower petals first, working from one cutting guide to the next; then return to the first cutting guide and add the foliage.

FLOWER HEADS

Begin with cutting guide No.1 and outline the very back petal on each flower head. Include extensions to fit behind the two adjacent petals.

Outline the top petal of each flower head on cutting guide No.2. Include extensions to fit behind the petal shapes that sit in front.

Outline the two central petals as one piece on cutting guide No.3. Include an extension to fit behind the bottom petal.

Finally, outline the bottom petals on cutting guide No.4; these pieces lay on top of the other petals so they do not require extensions.

FOLIAGE

Go back to cutting guide No.1 and outline the two leaves at the bottom of the picture. They sit below the flower head when the picture is assembled, so include extensions to fit behind the adjacent petals.

Outline the two stems on cutting guide No.2. Again, they are behind the other parts of the picture, so include extensions on each.

Outline the tiny turnover on the left-hand leaf on cutting guide No.3.

Outline the grasses on cutting guide No.4, with an extension to fit behind the right-hand flower.

REFERENCE NUMBERS

When I have identified all the shapes, I number them in the order of assembly. I then write the numbers on the back of the cut-out pieces as a cross-reference for when I build the picture.

Cutting guide No.1

Cutting guide No.2

Cutting guide No.3

Cutting guide No.4

Pansies

This pansy design has been enhanced with co-ordinating mount boards to give it a stunning appearance. I used five prints to create this three-dimensional image. A sixth, reference, print is always useful, and I usually glue this to the back of the framed picture. The raised areas of the design have been given a coat of cold glaze to make the flower heads appear to be made from fine porcelain.

Poppies

A step-by-step project with prints

Flowers are a fascinating subject to work with. They are my personal favourite as they can be sculpted to look so realistic that it is often difficult to tell that they are made from paper. Floral designs can be very simple or extremely complex and thus they are suitable for all levels of ability.

Many artists are now being commissioned to paint designs for three-dimensional découpage, and Lesley Teare, a very talented artist, painted this arrangement of poppies especially for this project. I have included six prints at the end of the book for you to use for this step-by-step project.

I have prepared a set of cutting guides to help you get started. All the pieces needed to complete the picture can be cut from just four of the prints. I have included extensions where necessary and I have numbered the pieces in their order of assembly. These numbers are referred to in the step-by-step instructions on pages 18–22. I have also marked the guides with small dots to indicate the position of the blobs of glue. Use the fifth print as the base print and the sixth print as a reference copy.

You could try making your own set of guides. To do this, first study the print to determine the different layers. Look at the bottom poppy and note how the darker green leaves and the stalks are at the very back of the design. Moving forward, the lime green leaf creates another layer. Next comes the two large petals at the back of the flower head, followed by the lower front petal and, finally, the upper front petal which is at the very front of the design.

The other poppy and foliage have a similar series of layers beginning with the top right-hand bud.

You will need:
The prints
Scissors or a craft knife
Envelopes for storing the shapes
Watercolour paints
Paint brush
Soft moulding mat
Moulding tool
Base board
Glue stick
Silicone glue

Cutting guide No.1

Cutting guide No.2

Cutting guide No.3

Cutting guide No.4

For shapes like the poppy centre (12), make a rough cut round the outside then remove fine triangles to create pointed spikes.

Step 1

Refer to the cutting guides on page 17 and then cut out the shapes from the prints. Cut cleanly round all outside edges and do not leave any background colour on the leaves or petals.

Cut fine details, such as the butterfly's antennae (20) slightly wider than they actually are so they do not break off.

Step 2

Number the back of the shapes lightly with a pencil. Keep the pieces cut from each print in separate envelopes.

Gently pinch the tips of the leaves to make more realistic shapes.

Step 3

Carefully mask the white edges of all the cut-outs using a small brush and a suitable watercolour paint. If paint strays on to the coloured image, wipe it away immediately.

Step 4

Shape the petals and leaves. Place a cut shape, print side down, on the moulding mat and run the handle of the scissors, or a moulding tool, over the back of the shape. Press gently into the mat. The double-petal pieces need concave shaping – mould them as above, then turn them over and press down on the centre of the shape to make the edges rise up on each side.

Step 5

Smooth a glue stick over the reverse side of the base print and stick it centrally to the base board.

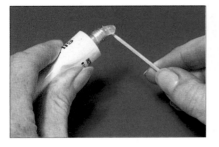

The shapes are assembled with balls of silicone glue – the larger the ball the higher the pieces will stand up. Use a cocktail stick to take the glue from the tube to the shapes.

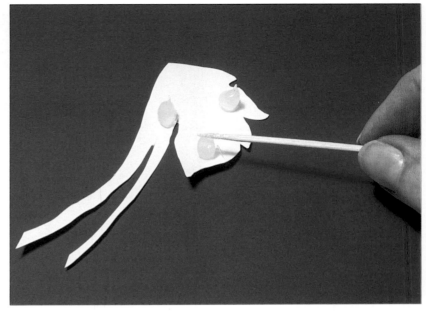

Step 6

Place three pea-sized blobs of glue on to the leaf/stem shape (1). Pull each ball of glue into points; when the piece is dropped into position, these points will sink slightly.

Hold your picture up in front of you from time to time to check that each piece is positioned correctly. Remember that this is how it will be seen on the wall.

Step 7

Use tweezers to position the piece on the base print. Match it as closely as you can to the image below. Do not press down or you will lose the three-dimensional effect.

Step 8

Build up the other background foliage by gluing and positioning pieces 2–9 on to the base print. Turn the base print round as you work on different areas to avoid knocking the other pieces out of position.

Step 9

Begin to assemble the upper flower head. Lay the moulded large back petal (10) face up and gently press it down in the centre to create a concave shape. Apply four blobs of glue to the piece and position it carefully on the base print, covering the extensions on the foliage below.

Step 10

Shape the front petals (11) as described in step 9. Apply two blobs of glue, then place this piece on top of the first petals. Use your reference print to check its position.

Step 11

Apply a single blob of glue to the middle of the spiky stamen piece (12). Place the stamen on top of the petals.

Step 12

Mould the central seed head (13) into a dome shape and glue it into position over the stamens.

Step 13

Assemble the two pieces of the butterfly (14 and 15). Bend the top wings slightly upwards to give depth to the image.

Step 14

Finally, assemble the bottom flower head, using pieces 16–20. Work in the same way as the upper one. Note that the top front petal (20) should be left as a convex shape. Set the assembled picture aside until the glue is completely dry then clean any excess glue from the base print and/or the individual shapes by rubbing lightly with your fingertips.

Opposite
The finished poppy picture
You can make the image look really stunning by applying a coat of cold glaze to the design. Protect the base print with scrap pieces of paper. Brush a thin coat of glaze on to the raised pieces, let it dry and then add a second coat.
You can customise the design to make it truly unique – include more spiky stamens in the centres of the flower heads, for example, or add an extra butterfly.

Adding detail

When you start to work on more complex designs realism often becomes of paramount importance. Here are just a few ideas that you might like to try when a design includes leaves and stems.

Accentuate the veins in a leaf by running along them gently with an embossing tool. Work on a spongy mould mat and do not press too hard or you will break the surface of the print.

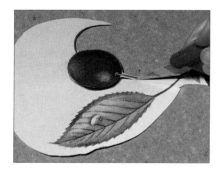

Use a craft knife to cut thin stalks and fronds slightly wider than they actually are and paint the white edges to match the printed colour.

Strengthen the stalks by applying a coat of PVA glue on the back.

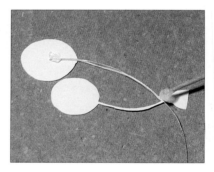

Another way of strengthening stalks is with fine florist's wire. Secure the wire with tiny blobs of silicone glue every 20mm (¾in).

Dewdrops on leaves and petals can be treated in different ways. You can cut a dewdrop from a second print, mould it and then position it on the leaf with a pin dot of glue (left). Alternatively, dry a small blob of silicone glue on a plastic sheet, ease it off with a knife and then position it with more glue (right). A tiny bead could also be used to create a different effect.

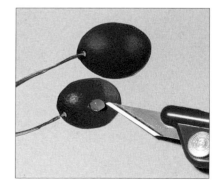

Cherries
I used the techniques shown opposite to create this three-dimensional image.
Note the difference between the dewdrops on the leaves and that on the cherry.

Enhancing a design

Never limit yourself to the printed image alone –
you will be amazed at what can be added to your
design to make it truly unique. It could be a tiny
twig, some beads or perhaps seeds from the spice
rack. Cake decoration shops stock a lovely
selection of artificial stamens and flower centres,
and you can find imitation moss and grasses in
modelling shops.

   The following pages contain examples of designs
that I have enhanced with items that can be found
in the home and garden.

*A selection of items that you can use to enhance a
design – artificial moss, sewing threads, twine, glitter
glue, sequins, glass beads, small fir cones, dressmaker's
pins, artificial stamens, poppy seeds, pencil shavings,
peppercorns, cardamom pods and caraway seeds.*

ENHANCED FLORAL

This design has a very textured appearance, which I enhanced with a variety of items. These were attached with tiny amounts of PVA glue.

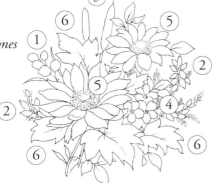

Key to diagram

1. *Small fir cones, painted to match the printed colours, replace the printed ones*
2. *Cardamom pods, painted pink, replace the seeds on some of the branches*
3. *Fine pencil shavings give texture to the long thin grasses*
4. *Small glass beads cover the centre of this flower*
5. *Painted poppy seeds cover the centre of this flower*
6. *Dried sage is used to add texture to the leaves*

Fuchsia

You can buy artificial stamens in various colours and sizes. White ones, painted to match the design, were used on this fuchsia. When the paint was dry, I shaped the stamens and then used small blobs of silicone glue to attach them to the underside of the petals.

Daisies

I added texture to the centres of these daisies by pricking them with a needle – obviously the thicker the needle, the larger the holes, so experiment on a piece of scrap print. Place the piece, printed side down, on a moulding mat and prick through from the back until you have created the effect you require. This technique also works very well on sunflowers.

Tulip

I enhanced the centres of these tulips with fennel seeds which are the correct shape and colour. I stuck each one into position using a tiny drop of glue.

I also added a gold bead to the centre of the tiny blue flowers. The easiest way to do this is to pick up the bead with a cocktail stick, touch the bead on a blob of glue and then drop it into the centre of the flower head. The cocktail stick should pull away cleanly.

Poinsettia

The spice cupboard provided the centre for this lovely deep red poinsettia. I placed glue in the centre of the assembled flower head and then dropped some coriander seeds into place.

Iris

I used tiny pieces of fur fabric to create the raised, soft centre of the iris. They were cut to shape, painted and then stuck into position.

Camellia

I used bought stamens for the centre of this camellia. Again I used white ones which I then painted to match the design. When they were dry, I tied them together in bunches and then cut them to the correct length. Stamens also make wonderful antennae for butterflies and other insects.

Varying the background

My favourite way of working floral designs and subjects like these butterflies, is to omit the base print and create an image that can be placed on a variety of backgrounds.

The base print is placed inside a clear plastic bag and the image is then assembled on to the plastic. The initial background pieces should be glued directly on to the plastic bag, but all of the other pieces must be glued in such a way that they become linked together. If every piece is only attached to the base, the design will fall apart when you move it.

Images created by this method are far more realistic than multi-layered designs and they also look more delicate. With this technique you can add more shape to the individual components as they do not have to match their positions on the original print.

The pictures on pages 31 and 32 show the same three-dimensional image on different backgrounds.

Insert the base print in a clear plastic bag or folder as a reference while you are building up the design.

Assemble the background pieces on to the plastic bag with silicone glue. If you want to angle a piece of the design, prop it with a small strip of foam board or balsa wood until the glue is dry.

Link all the layers together with blobs of glue. Here, I am linking an assembled butterfly to the background pieces with three blobs of glue.

Allow the completed design to dry and then use a flat kitchen knife to ease it away from the plastic.

You should be able to lift the design as a complete unit which you can then attach to a background of your choice with more glue. Remember, the larger the blobs of glue you use, the more the design will stand proud of the background.

30

Butterflies
Here, I have assembled the butterflies on a background of black velvet to give a very rich,
slightly Japanese feel to the design. Compare this with the same image on other backgrounds overleaf.

BACKGROUNDS

There are lots of materials that you can use as the background for your three-dimensional image.

Art shops and picture framers normally stock a wide range of coloured mount board. You could paint your own background on a sheet of watercolour paper. You could even use pieces of wallpaper pasted down on to mount board.

On this page, the butterfly image is shown on four different backgrounds. Note the subtle changes in the arrangement of the design – these occur because the image is flexible and takes on a slightly different shape each time it is moved.

*I sponged the background for this large picture, using pink and pale blue watercolours to imitate the background on the print.
For the three small versions below I used textured wallpaper (left), mottled mount board (centre) and smooth wallpaper (right).*

Mixing images

When you have perfected the technique of creating a picture without a static background, you can become really creative. You do not have to limit yourself to the design on a single print. You can let your imagination go and build up your own unique creation using the printed images from a selection of different subjects. This technique allows you to develop lots of depth in the picture.

The bouquet shown on pages 34–35 is made in this way. It is a mixture of flowers and foliage that were taken from a wide selection of prints, some of which are reproduced here.

This free-design technique works wonderfully well in a fire screen or even under a recessed glass table top.

Bouquet of mixed images
I used lots of different prints for this bouquet.
I made up the individual flower heads and areas
of foliage on plastic and allowed them to dry. I then
arranged them in the crescent design. To add extra detail
I included more tiny fronds and grasses cut from other prints and,
as a final finishing touch, I added two beautiful blue butterflies. This
type of work looks very effective when framed with a deep-recessed mount.

Variations

You do not have to limit yourself to making three-dimensional pictures; you can use individual flowers in lots of different ways; here are just two examples.

Add a wonderful finishing touch to a special gift by decorating the wrapping paper with three-dimensional découpage. In this example, I cut the roses and fine foliage from a print and made them up as a small bouquet on a sheet of plastic. I left it to dry and then I stuck the arrangement on the wrapping paper together with a tiny curl of ribbon to match that around the package.

I made a smaller arrangement which I attached to a handmade gift tag. You could also make a greetings card in the same way.

This is another way of putting three-dimensional découpage to good use.
I used the same print of roses to decorate both this picture frame and the parcel opposite .

Patching out

Scenes with lots of obvious layers and clearly defined edges make excellent subjects, and the picture opposite is a good example. They look best when they are worked as deeply-recessed pictures but, often, they can be spoiled by the duplication of the same image on different layers.

I have developed a method for overcoming this problem. I mask out foreground images from the background layers using two techniques: flat patching and raised patching. Sometimes, patching out can look a little untidy, but when the image is complete, nobody ever notices.

This window scene is typical of a landscape that can be made more realistic by patching out. I wanted to create an uninterrupted view through the window so I had to obliterate the window frame, the kettle and the vase from the layers in the background.

When working on designs like this, try to visualise the real scene. This will help you angle different areas of the picture to create a very realistic image.

FLAT PATCHING

I use flat patching for areas with minimal texture – skies, lawns, china, etc., and I sponge-paint the area to be masked or I paste down torn patches of paper taken from scrap pieces of the prints.

RAISED PATCHING

Raised patching is used for textured areas of the picture such as trees and foliage. I cut out the same piece from several prints and stick them over the area to be masked with PVA.

On the three-dimensional image, the window frame is built up well forward of the sky so I needed to mask it out of this first layer. I sponged the wooden frame with a fairly dry sky colour. Never get a print too wet or it will cockle.

On this middle distance layer, the kettle is still too prominent. To mask it out I tore up pieces of the path and grassy areas from other prints (see also page 40) and pasted them over the kettle. Apply patches with care, so that they only just cover the area to be masked. This way, the edge of the patch will look like a shadow on the completed picture.

Country view with kettle
This picture has lots of obvious layers and depth, making it an ideal subject for making into a deeply-recessed image. I used a number of patching-out techniques to mask out images from the background layers. I used eight prints to complete this three-dimensional picture.

Trees have lots of texture so I was able to use raised patches to cover the intrusive frame. I cut out clusters of leaves from scrap prints, moulded them and then built them up in layers to give the tree some depth.

The kettle also appears on these shutters. I cut some plain brown louvres from scrap prints and used them to cover the kettle. I glued them, together with the other louvres, at a slight angle to create the correct louvred effect.

Waterfront

A STEP-BY-STEP PROJECT

This lovely print is ideal for a deeply-recessed project; it has a number of very obvious layers, from the distant horizon through to the boats on the river. I show you how to build up these layers, step by step, and how to use patching-out techniques to make the finished picture look realistic.

I used ten prints to complete the picture, but the number you use will depend on how accurate you are when cutting out the pieces, and how many mistakes you make! Keep one extra print at your side as a reference.

I often use strips of foam board, rather than lots of glue, to raise layers of the image on deeply-recessed pictures.

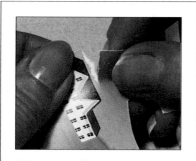

Tearing patches
When making a flat patch, pull each piece towards you so that the torn edge has no white paper showing on the coloured side. Remove the back layers of paper to make the pieces as thin as possible.

Step 1

Cut a piece of mount board, 20mm (¾in) larger all round than the print. Cut the sky area, with an extension into the sea below, from one print and stick it to the top of the board with a glue stick.

Step 2

Cut out all the clouds with small extensions into the sea. Mould them slightly and glue them over their respective images with small blobs of silicone glue. Cut out a few more clouds from another print and assemble them together to make a shape large enough to cover the image of the lighthouse. Glue this down with a couple of blobs of silicone glue.

Step 3

Cut out the sea with an extension that includes the distant hill at the left-hand side, and the row of houses below it. Tear flat patches of sea colour from other prints and, using PVA glue, patch out the image of the lighthouse and the house behind it. Patch just up to the edge of the image being covered – if you stray out too far on either side the patch will look very obvious.

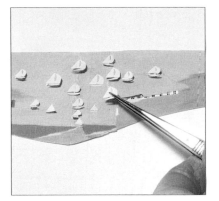

Step 4

Cut out the little boats and stick them down over their images on the sea with tiny blobs of silicone glue. Cut a few extra boats from another print and use them to disguise the lines of the patches.

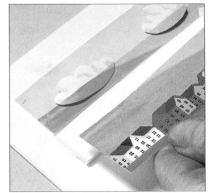

Step 5

Glue the completed sea area square to the horizon line. You could use blobs of glue, but I find that a strip of foam board or balsa wood, cut to the width of the picture, gives an even lift all the way along. Fix the strip to the base board using a glue stick.

Step 6

Cut out the distant left-hand hillside and row of houses (including an extension into land and sea below). Cut out patches of the hill colour from another print making them look like other layers of hills.

Step 7

Use PVA glue to stick the fake hills down over the top of the row of houses.

Step 8

Position the completed hill on the picture, so that the top of it is just proud of the horizon line, and the right-hand point is angled down to the sea.

Step 9

Use the images on two prints to cut out the individual houses, each with extensions on the left and bottom edges. Work from the right-hand side and glue the houses together, overlapping where there are extensions. Add fine details, such as gables, windows and roofs, cut from scrap pieces of print.

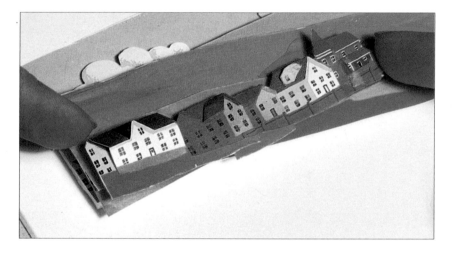

Step 10

Glue the complete row of buildings on to the picture over the patched-out hill. Angle them upwards, so they are just proud of the surface of the hill.

Step 11

Cut out the length of the harbour wall with an extension that includes the middle-distance hill at the left across to the point where the hill meets the sea. To complete the piece, cut the bottom of the sea wall along the water's edge. Cut the tiny boats from another print and glue them on to the wall with tiny blobs of silicone glue. Apply blobs of silicone to the wall and place it in position so that its bottom edge touches the sea area.

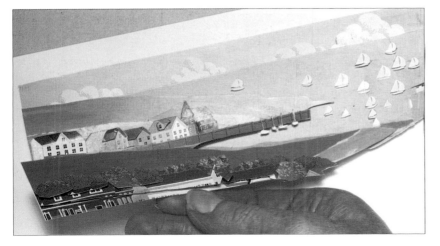 

Step 12

Cut out the middle distance hill, including an extension into the houses below. Cut out the bushes from another print and glue over their images on the hill. Cut out extra bushes from scrap pieces of print and use these to cover the chimney pots and the roofs of the houses. Add the completed hillside to the picture.

Step 13

Make up the lighthouse and the buildings behind it, adding extra detail around the light at the top. Glue the buildings and then the lighthouse to the picture.

Step 14

Add more layers of foam board to make a base for the middle-distance images. Stagger the height so that there is more at the left-hand side – visually, the building at centre right is further back than those at the left.

Step 21

Make up the harbour wall from two prints. Use the right-hand side of each print to make a wall that is free from boat images. Cut posts from other prints and glue these to the wall to add relief. Glue the wall to the angled road parallel to the base. Support it until the glue is dry.

Step 22

Cut out the foreground area of water. For this piece, which will tuck under the harbour wall, include an extension on the top edge. From spare prints cut out swirls of water and use these to patch out the images of the boats on the river, and to give more texture to all the water.

Step 23

Glue the water shape under the harbour wall, angling it up towards you. Support it with a piece of foam board as shown.

Step 24

Finally, make up the boats and wire the masts for added strength (see page 24). Glue them into position with their sterns touching the water.

Below
Waterfront
The finished picture before mounting. I built a box frame (painted green to match the picture) tight up to the sides of this image before framing it (see page 58).

Adding texture

I have already touched on the subject of adding texture to floral designs, but there really is no limit to the application of texture. Here are a few more ideas that you might like to incorporate in your work.

INTO THE WOOD

I love this design, and it offers a lot of opportunities for adding texture and interest and so bringing the scene to life.

The finished three-dimensional picture (opposite) was worked on a base print. I patched out the sledge, rabbit and mouse using torn paper and the flat patching technique. The tiny hedgehog was masked out with the base of another tree taken from a scrap of print. Artificial moss was used to cover the join.

As usual, I started building up the three-dimensional image from the back of the picture.

I spent a long time adding lots of fine detail to the forest.

I made up separate three-dimensional images of the sledge full of parcels and the individual animals. I allowed them to dry completely before adding them to the picture.

Finally, I added the log and the snowy hillside at the front.

I created the moss among the trees from fine pencil shavings. You could use artificial moss available from modelling shops.

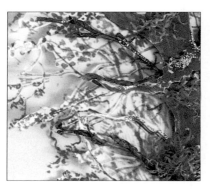

I added some real twigs to give depth to the forest. Collect only very fine twigs. Ensure that they are dry before attaching them with silicone glue.

I made up the sledge and its contents as a separate three-dimensional image which I then glued in position. I cut the tiny strap from a piece of leather, stuck the paper buckle on top and then glued the strap to the sledge.

I used ordinary sewing thread for the whiskers on the animals. I dipped the thread in PVA glue, wiped off the excess with my finger tips and allowed the thread to dry. To make the fine cotton easier to handle, I attached over-length pieces with more PVA glue, and then trimmed them to size. I also used the same thread to enhance the fine grasses in the foreground.

Opposite
Into the woods
The finished picture.

I created the icy effect in the forest, on the sledge and on the edges of the snow with glitter glue. I added glitter gradually to build up the sheen. I also added small glass beads on the animals' clothing.

I used a random pricking technique to create texture on the snowy hill in the foreground.

The snowman

This picture is by Anton Pieck, the prolific Dutch artist, who produced a wealth of designs which are now very popular subjects for three-dimensional découpage. He had a wonderful sense of perspective and his abundance of fine detail challenges découpage artists the world over. Sadly he did not live long enough to see the excitement his work has created.

This design has a lot of intricate detail in it and is composed of three obvious areas: the background consists of the little village and the trees; the middle ground is the ice rink; and the foreground is composed of the tree, the snowman, the children and the dog.

I created a new sky area by sponging a piece of white board to give the correct colouring. I built the village on a piece of plastic, adding glitter to the houses and trees to give a frosty sparkle. When it was dry I assembled the village on to the background with silicone glue.

I flat patched the skating rink, then 'stood' the skaters on it. I assembled the ice rink on the base board at an angle, supporting it with a strip of foam board.

I patched out the characters from the front area of the small hill, added texture to the snow using the pricking technique and then spread glitter glue over the snow to give it a sparkle. I strengthened the tree trunk and branches with wire, and then moulded them to stand proud. Finally, I made up the snowman and the children and positioned them at the correct angle.

Figures

Designs that include figures often lend themselves to being made into greetings cards as well as pictures. They are a delight to work with as the component shapes are relatively easy to define and cut out, and the figure can often be made to have a personality of its own. Here are a few points that will help you make your figures look more realistic.

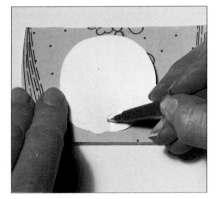

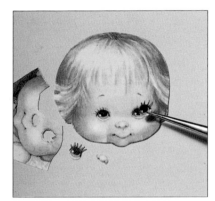

FACES
Use the smooth handles of your scissors to give a roundness to the face. When building the image on a base print, remember that heavy shaping can reduce the size of the piece of paper. Use an embossing tool to emphasise the cheeks. Do not press too hard with fine-pointed tools or you may break the surface of the print.

EYES AND NOSES
Cut eyes and noses from a separate print. Cut the eyelashes as finely as you can and paint them in with black paint. Create shape with a fine embossing tool.

HAIR
Cut out the complete hair shape roughly and then, working from the outer edge inwards, cut into the shape to create the fine strands of hair. Make sure each strand has a pointed tip by removing fine slivers of paper.

CLOTHING
Accentuate clothing by moulding and layering. The dress featured in this picture has lots of folds and frills. Cut more frills from other prints and emboss them to accentuate the shape. Add more layers to the skirt to increase the depth of the image.

Holly Days
This cute design of an angel could be made into a special Christmas card. For this
finished image I used five prints and assembled the pieces on a sheet of plastic over a reference
print. I added lots of definition to the holly leaves and moulded the berries with a fine
embossing tool to make them well rounded. I also added extra folds to the skirt to
increase the depth of the image.

DREAMING ABOUT TOMORROW

This design is an ideal subject for the nursery. There are lots of obvious layers, the shapes are relatively simple to work with and there is plenty of detail that can be used to good effect.

Patching out the bed cover allows adjustments to be made to the positions of the animals on the bed thereby adding to the perspective.

I used five prints to make the completed picture opposite.

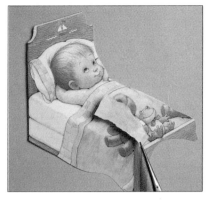

I used the flat patching technique to create an uninterrupted blue bed cover. I tore pieces of the side of the bed cover from other prints and used these to mask out the images of the animals on the top. I shaped and then positioned the pieces to make them appear as folds in the material.

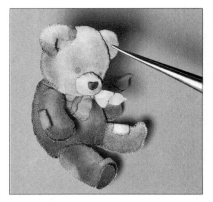

I added lots of detail on the teddy bears and the frog, each of which I assembled on plastic before adding to the design. I created the effect of fur by fringing – making lots of tiny cuts in the outer edges of each bear.

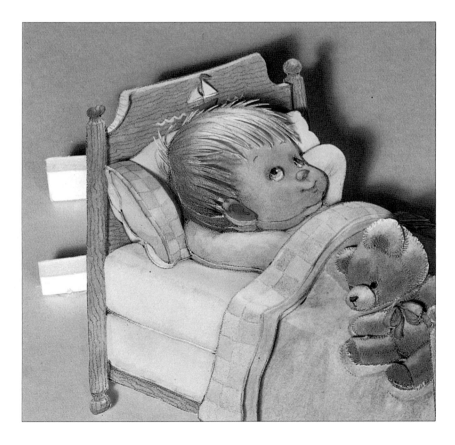

I assembled the complete picture on plastic and then transferred it on to a plain cream background. To emphasise the perspective, I used strips of foam board placed under the headboard to lift the design up from the background.

Opposite
Dreaming about tomorrow
The finished picture.

School days

*I emphasised the fur of the teddy and the tiny mouse by making a series of fine spiky cuts around
the edges of the shapes. I used a knife to cut out the areas between the wrought iron to give a delicate but
realistic appearance. I decided to change the background colour from white to blue, so I built
up the image on plastic and then glued it on to a new base. I applied selective glazing, limiting it to
the iron work, the items on the desk and the teddies' eyes – I do not usually glaze anything furry.*

56

Balancing clown
*I changed the background of this picture to contrast with the bright colours
of the clown. I used crochet cotton for the yo-yo string and real
ribbon for the bows on the shoes. This design is one of a series of
four clown pictures which can look very effective when made up
and framed together in pairs.*

Mounting and framing

A special frame for a deeply-recessed picture can be expensive. But, if you build a box round your picture you can mount it in a normal frame. I use one of two basic methods depending on the type of picture to be framed.

OTHER IMAGES

If I am framing a floral design, for example, without a squared-up edge, I prefer not to see the recessed box. For these images the backing board must be the same size as the inner edge of the frame.

Set the mount board face down in the frame and then stick strips of double-sided tape round the inner edge of the frame. Cut strips of foam board to the required width and length, and then press them, edge down, on the tape to form a box-like structure.

DEEPLY-RECESSED SCENES

Images with considerable depth, especially those with straight-line edges to them, look better if they are presented with a box built tight up to the image.

I use strips of 5mm (¼in) thick foam board or balsa wood to box in the picture. I select balsa wood when I want to colour the box to match the picture.

Cut strips that are just wider than the depth of the picture. Size the lengths so that they can be butted together tightly at the corners. Glue each strip to the base board right up against the edge of the design. Check that there are no gaps. Allow to dry, then trim off any excess base board.

Cut a mount to size and then fix it against the glass in the frame with staples. Position the mount over the design and hold it up in front of you to check its position. When you are satisfied, tape the boxed picture to the back of the mount with masking tape.

Screw eye hooks into the wood (not the boxed image) and string with picture wire.

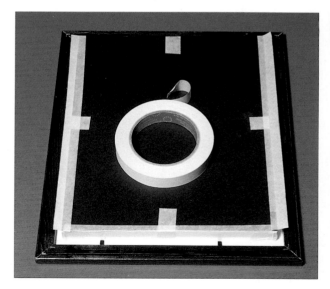

Place the completed three-dimensional picture face down on the box and attach it with masking tape.

Take time to choose mount boards and frames that will complement your finished pictures.

Gallery

On the next few pages I have included a few of my favourite subjects. Some, like the one on this page, are quite complex while others are relatively simple in their construction.

Cats in focus

This picture is one of the most challenging designs I have ever worked on and remains a firm favourite. I used ten prints to make this image.

I re-upholstered the screen in the background using a printed dress fabric. I stiffened the fabric with thin card, added the woodwork, and then bent it in and out to create the correct shaping. I used the same technique for the rug to which I then added a fringe made from a tassel.

I patched out the cats where necessary and then made them up individually. I used bristles cut from a clothes brush for their whiskers.

I made the satin-covered ledge by covering a piece of foam board with gold satin fabric. First, I stitched fine pleats into the material then wrapped it round the foam board and secured it at the top and bottom with glue. Finally, I adjusted the gathers to create the correct effect. This was especially important where the cat is peeping underneath it. I filled the planters with imitation moss.

I used crochet cotton, stiffened with PVA glue, for the tangle of wires connecting the photographer's lamps.

I mounted the picture on a piece of plain white board and used strips of foam board to help build up the depth.

Opposite and above
Peach roses and camellias
Both of these florals were made up on plastic, using a print for reference. They were then moved to different backgrounds to create unusual effects. By using this method I was able to shape the leaves and petals to make them look very realistic, and to lift each layer to make images with considerable depth. I gave both images a coat of cold glaze to give them the look of porcelain.

Polar bears

A number of techniques was used to bring this delightful polar bear picture to life. The sea was cut out and angled forward to give the correct perspective. The bears were patched out by cutting lots of extra areas of snow. These were pricked and then added to the design to give extra texture to the landscape. The edges of the bears were cut fairly deeply to denote shaggy fur. Once complete, the design was given an icy finish using glitter glue.

Opposite
Rock-a-bye bears clock
The découpage design was made up using five prints, one of which was used for reference. Each part of the design had to be carefully secured to the other parts during construction. The pine base and clock mechanism were purchased from a craft outlet and assembled according to instructions. Blobs of silicone glue hold the rocking horse in position and a coat of cold glaze gives it both protection and a shine.

Oriental girl
This three-dimensional image of a Japanese lady was created by Joanne Hewitt. It has been made up
on a base print as the delicate background would be difficult to recreate. The designs on the dress and the
vase have been raised. Lots of detail has been added to the flowers and trees. This design requires six prints.

Summer hamper
This is an ideal and unusual design for the kitchen. The picture has been placed
on a mottled blue background. Extra fruits have been inserted to cover
any gaps – another patching-out technique.

Index

Project prints
Opposite, and on subsequent pages, you will find six prints for the step-by-step project given on pages 16–23. Do not tear the pages from the book as you may ruin the binding. Remove them by cutting along the broken line with a craft knife.